F[illegible]D
DROUGHT POETRY

Experiences of Weather Extremes in Staffordshire

Various Authors

Edited by

Mel Wardle Woodend, Dr Alice Harvey-Fishenden

and Professor Neil Macdonald

FLOOD AND DROUGHT POETRY – EXPERIENCES OF WEATHER EXTREMES IN STAFFORDSHIRE

First Printing: 2022

ISBN: 978-1-7397105-7-6 (DREAM WELL WRITING LTD)

DREAM WELL WRITING LTD

STAFFORDSHIRE

UNITED KINGDOM

www.dreamwellwriting.simplesite.com

DREAM WELL

A Dyslexia Friendly Publication

UNIVERSITY OF LIVERPOOL

UK CLIMATE RESILIENCE PROGRAMME

Staffordshire County Council

Staffordshire
History Centre

Staffordshire & Stoke on Trent
• Archive Service •

Flooding at the Green, Stafford, February 1946 (Image courtesy of Staffordshire Record Office and Peter Rogers)

CONTENTS

FOREWORD

The poems in this volume developed from a series of workshops organised by Mel Wardle Woodend on behalf of the 'Building Climate Resilience through Community, Landscapes and Cultural Heritage' (CLandage) project, in partnership with the Staffordshire Record Office. The poems were inspired by stories of past floods and droughts, from archival and newspaper sources, which were presented during the workshops.

The original research plan for the CLandage project was to develop a touring exhibition that would travel around the local archives and libraries of Staffordshire, from which public understanding and memories of the weather would have been gathered. However, the COVID pandemic of 2020 prevented this from happening, with many archives, museums and libraries closed or operating under limited access because of restrictions. This presented a challenge for the project in how best to engage with the people and communities of Staffordshire, when many were unable to leave their homes. A series of online poetry workshops, small creative workshops and outdoor creative writing and walking events were organised. This poetry book is the culmination of the online poetry workshops held through the period of COVID pandemic restrictions.

We thank all those who attended and contributed to the workshops, and other events, and whose work is presented within these pages. We would like to express our gratitude to the Arts and Humanities Research Council whose funding through grant AH/V003569/1 enabled this research to take place, as part of the UK Climate Resilience programme.

We would also like to take this opportunity to thank Mel Wardle Woodend for adapting, developing and running the poetry workshops. With special thanks to Helen Johnson and Matthew Blake from the Staffordshire Record Office; without their efforts CLandage and this poetry book would not have come about.

Professor Neil Macdonald and Dr Alice Harvey-Fishenden

School of Environmental Sciences,
University of Liverpool,
August 2022

NOTE FROM THE STAFFORDSHIRE POET LAUREATE

As soon as I received the first email from Helen Johnson at the Staffordshire Record Office telling me of their work with the University of Liverpool and the CLandage project and met with Professor Neil Macdonald and Dr Alice Harvey-Fishenden from the university on Zoom to learn more about the project, I knew this was going to be an exciting and engaging venture to be involved with.

I thoroughly enjoyed the research aspect of the preparation for the workshops: two of which would be on the theme of flood and two on the theme of drought, during which I learnt a great deal about Staffordshire history in terms of extreme weather events. Some of the events I drew on were from my own lifetime, and involved incidents I clearly remember, and some from decades or centuries ago with resources and materials provided by Dr Alice Harvey-Fishenden to help inform my poetry workshops.

The workshops themselves were a joy to deliver – and it was excellent to work with participants on Zoom who might otherwise have been unable to attend face to face workshops.

I feel the poetry that resulted from the workshop exercises, research materials and prompts is of an excellent quality and it is an honour to publish a selection of these poems in *Flood and Drought Poetry – Experiences of Weather Extremes in Staffordshire* through my small press Dream Well Writing Ltd. This poetry collection will enable others to read and learn about Experiences of Weather Extremes in Staffordshire through the voices of those who interpreted the workshop materials, resources and exercises to inspire their own poetry, and / or drew on their own experiences to create personal pieces of Flood and Drought Poetry.

Thank you to Helen, Neil and Alice for inviting me to deliver the poetry workshops and publish this anthology and for all the support you have given me in both preparation for the workshops, your attendance and participation at them, and your poetry contributions. Thank you also to all the participants of the workshops for their engagement and enthusiasm and for the beautiful poetry created, that has made this book possible.

Mel Wardle Woodend
Staffordshire Poet Laureate 2019-2022
Director of Dream Well Writing Ltd

FLOOD AND DROUGHT

WEATHER EXTREMES IN STAFFORDSHIRE

Poetry Workshops with
Staffordshire Poet Laureate
Mel Wardle Woodend
In Partnership with Staffordshire
Archives and Heritage Service and
Liverpool University - CLandage Project

'When the Rain Came' - Flood Part 1 23/6/21 10.00 - 12.00
Exploring flood through visual images, shared experiences, and poetry examples to inspire Choka poetry or a shape poem.

'When the Rain Came' - Flood Part 2 30/6/21 10.00 - 12.00
Using visual images, written records, and personal experiences to inspire poetry on flooding in Staffordshire from a variety of perspectives.

'When There Wasn't Water' - Drought Part 1 7/7/21 10.00 - 12.00
Exploring drought in Staffordshire through visual images, written records, own experiences, and poetry examples to create haiku poetry on the theme of drought.

'When There Wasn't Water' - Drought Part 2 14/7/21 10.00 - 12.00
Exploring a variety of written records of drought in Staffordshire and creating redacted poetry from these.

Free to attend. Please contact melwoodendwriting@gmail.com or 07581 244393 to book a place on Zoom

MEL WARDLE WOODEND AUTHOR AND POET

Staffordshire County Council

UNIVERSITY OF LIVERPOOL

UK CLIMATE RESILIENCE PROGRAMME

Staffordshire History Centre

'WHEN THE RAIN CAME'

FLOOD WORKSHOP 1

Exploring flood through visual images, shared experiences, and poetry examples to inspire Choka poetry or a shape poem.

A Water Droplet

A small
autumn raindrop falls,
soaking the ground, the soils take their fill,
quenching its thirst, excess waters begin to flow, plants
bend and release their hold, the silt rich waters begin to move,
water gurgles brown and coarse, building energy soon dispersed,
upon reaching road or path, releasing hold its grainy grasp,
casually dropped to be clasped again, when rains refreshed

True representation of a raindrop

Neil Macdonald

Blithfield in Drought and Flood

Deep-fathomed blueness
all consuming; runs its course;
legalised drowning
centuries swallowed up, whole.
Now; scorched earth searing.
In stillness, Yeatsall Hollow;
Blithfield Lodge - asleep;
its mill wheel bearing witness
to lives once lived here.
Then, quicksilver lightning flash;
vanishing card trick,
the wheel turns, and - poof! - is gone
as dark skies rain down their wrath.

Daralyn Hammond

Climate Change 'I Am Flood'

Relentless raining
incessant drip, drop, drip, drop
I slap the bare soil
racing home to my river
the hungry water swells
I roar, I roll and erupt
devouring the land
I stretch out and slow my pace
sated I stop now
landscape consumed by water
I reflect the sky
at peace now I drain away
my silty print stays
the sun warms me, and I float
upwards to the cloud
I wait, I grow, now heavy
cycle completed
I am ready drip, drop, drip
relentless raining – are you?

Dawn Pope

Doxey Road Long Stay Carpark

Lapping flood water
creeping across the carpark.
I search for dry ground,
avoid permanent puddles
(a flood plain does not
work well covered in tarmac)
I find a high point,
park on a ridge of pavement,
where water won't reach, today.

Alice Harvey-Fishenden

Flood on the Dove

Calm green meadows gone
a dim prelude to the town
lay still, sweet field, though
silent bird song resonates.
No melodic muse.
Buzzing insects' absence make
pillows for my woes.
Soundless skies speak by gone verse –
senseless, abstract - mine.

Peeking through my half-closed eyes
a coal pit lagoon
beckons, caressing my wounds
it's there I must go
yet eye lid wings flap open
lo, a golden moon
shining defiantly and
wind swept grasses join
to show me the light, right way.

But no half bitten
moon can brighten my doomful days
halting these dark skies
so vulgarly pretending
it could care for us.
You look down from your tower.
Warm now distant love
you gave then took away, yet
mine survived the storm
only to float away, covered
by God's midnight cloak.

You watch from your fortress high
as I share my soul
with the land that made me man
I doff my cap to
flood, field, forest and you,
who survived the storm – adieu.

Joanna Smart

Freeflowing

Freeflowing
surging
in ribbons
of
Red……Gold
Blue……Silver
in
Green…Bronze
Metallic
Elements

Weaving
Overtaking
Revolving
Treading
Converging
Clustering
Jamming
to
Pinch Point
Overlapping…
Flooding…
Drowning…

Jan Hedger

Lichfield (2018)

Wet pavements; cold feet;

so, lovely weather for ducks

but not for humans

huddling; shiv'ring in doorways.

And it does not stop

the rain; into Wetherspoons

fingers round hot drinks.

The bar is very crowded.

Babbling man, gin-soaked,

drowning in glass of amber.

Wet as the weather

maybe inwardly ponders

'sober' soon; I am

stone cold, but not hostile, though

don't speak his language.

No-one, no man, an island.

Let him be 'no threat'

I tell the waiter, smiling.

The man, he drinks on.

He needs firm ground; safe harbour;

thirst slaked - by a diff'rent cup...

Daralyn Hammond

Moorland Monsoon

The rain came early
that year the monsoon wind tore
from the South the West
Doxey Pool's cellophaned lid
stripped to tearing air
the raked hills the high moors next
water wall crashed hard
against Axe Edge's charred flanks
cascaded Chrome Hill's ridged ribs

supple bamboo groves
of Goldsytch Moss warned me first
the calm had stilled me
just cicadas snapped the hush
I drunk in the hush
smelt a crackle in my veins
electricity
tremble gentle then urgent
I looked up it had begun

long miles of bruised sky
a hare nosed the swelling sky
over Wales a war
high above the plain the same

gulls white refugees
ozone came in galleon holds
the gulls on currents
topaz clouds gunmetal too
horizon danced liquid flame

I was alone now
bamboo swaying in voodoo trance
ten thousand shamans
chanted ultramontane charms
green whipped stalks dancing
in the fields the soughs sighing
moaning yearning for
in the fields wired sheep churning
drumming rainfall full coming

Mark Johnson

Oceans Rise

I have seen my oceans rise through global warming.
I have seen the resulting devastating flooding.
I have seen my water ways contained and diverted
leaving arid lands and famine, the end of all life.
All done to feed the greedy wants of man.

My arteries are clogged with waste.
My waters polluted.
I have nowhere to go in man's concrete jungle.
So I must rail and fight against man's destructive force.
Death now to ensure life survives-to show the way.

Man rails and fights against the coming of the flood.
Rails against its mighty power.
They do not see the destructive power of greed and selfishness.
Men, do not fight and rail against the coming of the flood.
Rail and fight against the ignorance of man.

Heed my hard lessons. Learn before it is too late.

Patricia Pope

The Drowning

A
rib
bon
rib
bed
in
f
l
o
w
i
n
g
lines
so neatly
s
e
w
n
on to
banks
of bottle
green

grass
h p e
o p r
meadows
flush with
fine fIlaments of fauna
t h r e a d e d through.
Where larks
e
s
i
r
in
melodius
song
from surface nests
and a rich
s
e
a
m
of life

lays
buried
beneath.

From afar
swamped soil sobs,
its tears
torrential
t
u
m
b
l
e
towards this peaceful scene.

Slow, the silent, seeping, creeping fingers
of fraying ribbon rivulets onto sleeping fields
and small life, seemingly safe in secretly tunnelled homes,
is
quietly quenched.

Kathy Dowling

The Trent Flooding

When winter cloudbursts
of freshly wept tears rained down
rivers rose, water
swirling and bulging their banks
until they overflowed
bursting, releasing torrents
rushing across land
tilled, toiled and laboured over
all to no avail
fish hid in hollows, tree roots,
underneath eddies
for self-protection from harm.
Bracken breaks away
tench, perch, carp, roach, pike, dace, bream
young Sargasso Sea eels
swimming against the onslaught.
Freshwater sponges
shudder, clinging on to rocks.
Muddy flood waters
exert ferocious power
causing disorder
boats from their moorings are torn
cars are abandoned
but the mighty Trent moves on
carrying driftwood
wellington boots, old bicycles
travelling through shires
until it joins the river Ouse
and spills into the Humber

Christine Shaw

‘WHEN THE RAIN CAME’

FLOOD WORKSHOP 2

Using visual images, written records, and personal experiences to inspire poetry on flooding in Staffordshire from a variety of perspectives.

Astonfields Balancing Lakes

Once I was a flood meadow seasonally grazed by cattle.
Then the saltworks came, they drained my groundwaters and dumped their briny wastes upon my soil
neighbours planted trees to block their view of my blighted landscape
hidden between railway lines, housing and industrial estates I languished
winter came, I flooded. Summer came, I drained
vegetation caressed my soil once more
not ordinary seeds but specialised species that tolerate my salty soils
plants usually associated with the seaside thrive here with me.
The birds that brought these germs of hope now reside here within my brackish habitat
heron, teal & reed warblers.
I feature in bird guides now.
My north lake is glistening open water, home to luminous dragonfly and prattling ducklings
my south lake shyly hides her shimmering splendour being shrouded in saltmarsh flora.
I have survived exploitation and pollution and now I serve Stafford as a flood defence.
When rainwater rages, I smooth and buffer the torrent, releasing the manic surge only after it has rested and calmed.
I am Astonfields balancing lakes.
I am survival.

Dawn Pope

A Diary of Water

At almost the beginning of time I was gifted to you when the meteors rained down upon this pitiful parched proto planet.
Soon I shrouded this thin earthly crust, encasing that throbbing magma heart with my mighty oceans creating a truly blue planet.
I am water, the bearer of creation,
Life was sparked within me, simple single celled organisms. I provided both the medium for life and the reactant for photosynthesis that creator of oxygen.
This energy enabled organisms to grow and develop, creating wonderous and multifarious lifeforms, the descendants of which inhabit this planet today.
I am water, the bearer of life,
I stretch and layer forming fibrous fingers of frost which gripped this planet within my frozen fist. As I melted and shifted, I shaped the land beneath me.
I am water, the bearer of landscape.
Much time has now passed, and man has emerged, ancient civilisations have formed in my fertile crescents and now you pray to me that I should continue to nourish this land and replenish your potable reserves.
I am water, the bearer of hope.
Now it is the Anthropocene age and mankind has exerted its influence. You have drained my aquifers, dammed or diverted the flow of my mighty rivers and mutilated the soil so I cannot percolate homeward. When I break these puny confines, you fear me and call me flood.
I am water, the bearer of destruction.

Dawn Pope

A Sad Change in the Weather

From the diaries of Elizabeth Hervey (1748-1820)

It blew hard last night, and I slept ill, was unwell.
I heard the watchman at 4 o'clock, crying a fine morning
and when I rose, not a cloud was to be seen.
Yet if I had not walked early, I should not have got out at all
for as I walked clouds by degrees spread over the sky.
The wind cuts like a knife, a deplorable, doubtful day.
The late floods have done much mischief,
carrying away the gravel and a small rustic bridge
melancholy consequences must be expected for the harvest.
I am quite tired of such repeated rain,
although all weather seems alike to me
for scarcely one hour do I pass free from pain.

Alice Harvey-Fishenden

A Terraced House, Bolebridge Tamworth 1884

Martha lifted the guttering candle
as if in lifting it, she lifted herself
from the sepia sewage water
circling her heels, like a rabid dog
in high state of fever.

Biting cold as sharp as a rat's bite,
guttersnipes with black eyes,
she feared rats above anything else;
feared rats even more than the filth
at her laced booted feet.

Martha pinched her nose with
her free hand, mouth shut tight
trying to curb the stench from
flooding her aged lungs,
the Tame on her tongue.

Shouts, cries from the street,
a bell ringing 'unclean, unclean'.
'Evacuate! Evacuate! All tenants to leave.
Evacuate! All tenants to leave.
Bring no possessions!'

Martha tied in her woollen shawl,
as if tying it in would keep her safe,
extinguished the candle, hitched
up her linen skirt and tip-toed
through the rising menace.

Poem based on article accessed at http://www.patrickcomerford.com/2016/06/guys-almshouse-tamworth-legacy-with.html

Jan Hedger

A Thief in the Night

Rain sweeps in,
blows out the lamplight -

a thief in the night takes a chance
runs free
          black bellied and cold
it runs through the streets
swells and spews
through doors
eats its fill of concrete and cobbles

and life
falls into the pits
of its belly

it sits
bulging
unmoved
a swamp at the ankles
of houses.

Claire Hughes

Rain

Raging torrents of water, falling from the sky.

Aiming towards the ground, filling rivers and drains spilling over fields and towns.

Innocent people terrified moving belongings, mortified.

'Never again' they cry, feeling heartache at ruined treasures.

Next season they hope for better defences to be rid of their plight.

Patricia Wardle

The Turn of Day

I stand at the bedroom window,
        watch the clouds
darken, as if they are soaking
up an ink spill;

        watch the sun
retreat   fear sodden;

        watch the rain
fall and scatter   slow at first
then the sky splits and spits water
out like bullets.

        My land   the Earth
buckles under the strain,
bleeds brown mulch,
the flood   an open wound.

        I watch
as my flock are carried off,
one by one,
to a distant dream.

        I watch
the harvest fall
into the mouth of the gods

        And I watch
the tyrannical hand of nature
reclaim what is hers.

        I watch
my life melt into the overgrown river
and wonder how to swim.

Claire Hughes

OTHER FLOOD POETRY

Haiku and More

A Lovely Cup of Tea

Factual Haiku water footprint of black tea

One cup of tea needs
thirty litres of water.
Anyone want milk?

Dawn Pope

Catchment Area

How neatly mapped
the watershed.
How clean the lines
that dole responsibility
from one authority
to the other.
And oh! How
omniscient
the force
of gravity
that rules all
from high to low.
It *shall* go down:
water *will* proceed
according to the law.
But what if
that law
does not fit
the lie
of the land?
Or if by
man's hand
the lie

of the land

is altered;

old watercourses

falter

and new arise?

Perhaps

the defendant

has an alibi.

Perhaps he

acted without

ill intent –

did not mean

to commit an

offence. But

ignorance of

the law

is no defence;

will make

floodwaters

no less intense;

will prove

as powerless

as a sandbagged fence.

Mark Johnson

Cows Lie Down

Cows lie down chewing,
a sign that weather beckons.
Rain sweeps over them.

Christine Shaw

Historical Poem

Carriage rocks, horse whinnies in worry,

waters surge, rising higher,

ford's centre nears, whinnies now a crying,

pushing forward, load unmoved,

waters lower, whinnies now subsiding,

breathing deep, dry land, relax.

Neil Macdonald

The Reservoir

Under deep water
unknown fathoms; the bells toll
lost Sundays at church

Daralyn Hammond

Vicarage Flood

In 1999
deep water inundated
the Vicarage garden.

The Forebridge drain rose.
It flooded our garden room
to a foot or so.

The water was clean
because we discovered we
had a flood barrier.

Thankfully not mud
and mess and raw brook sewage.
Neither smell nor stinks.

The barrier kept
the water out so that it
seeped up through the ground.

When the waters left
things returned back to normal
after drying out.

Our neighbours had planned
daughter's wedding reception
in a big marquee.

The waters fell back
and the event was unharmed.
A joyful result.

Based on personal experiences

Beryl Metcalf

Water Gushing Down

Water gushing down.

Firemen rushing to rescue.

All is calm at last.

Patricia Wardle

Note: My Mum wrote this haiku for me a couple of weeks after the workshops when a pipe burst on the 12th floor of my building and torrents of water flooded down the internal airvents and outside of the building.

Although a different cause of flood than the extreme weather events discussed in the workshops, when the firemen attended I explained the irony of having not long delivered a set of poetry workshops about floods! – Mel Wardle Woodend

'WHEN THERE WASN'T WATER'

DROUGHT WORKSHOP 1

Exploring drought in Staffordshire through visual images, written records, own experiences, and poetry examples to create haiku poetry on the theme of drought.

A Bow of Promise

Heat unrelenting,
a Bow of Promise glinting,
fresh relief envied.

A 'Bow of Promise' was an alternative name for a rainbow in the Victorian period, associated with the biblical context (Genesis 9:13) as a promise never to send a flood again.

Neil Macdonald

A Hot Desert Wind

A hot desert wind

the Sirocco from Africa

blows oppressively.

Christine Shaw

Drought

Scorched riverbed lies
like a withered, fissured tongue
in death's gaping mouth

Kathy Dowling

Drought

Dirty dry doldrums
heat halving hotting harvest
heralding hunger.

Clay cracked the brickwork
when the sun shone seamlessly
on the dry earth. (1976)

In the caravan
stifling heat and closed windows
to exclude biters.

Bewildering worries
wrack wondering wanderers.
Do we have a home?

Berkshire gear breakdown.
Brother rescues family
A34 help.

Our house cracked right down both side walls in 1976 due to clay shrinkage. We took the children round Europe for 6 weeks in the summer of 1983 while it was underpinned.

Beryl Metcalf

Drought Walsall (1976)

Clay cracked the brickwork

when the sun shone seamlessly

on the dry earth.

Beryl Metcalf

Inexhaustible

Water exhausted

by selfish green grass addicts

and a long dry spell

Alice Harvey-Fishenden

Lightning Reaction

Lightning reaction
striking Earth like Thor's hammer
makes heavy weather

Christine Shaw

Water Tap Splutters

water tap splutters

a s t a c c a t o tympani

– oh! Dry summer cough...

Mark Johnson

'WHEN THERE WASN'T WATER'

DROUGHT WORKSHOP 2

Exploring a variety of written records of drought in Staffordshire and creating redacted poetry from these.

Do People Think Heatwaves Are Un-British

[redacted] un-British?

[redacted]

[redacted] a small boy ran into the street and started to dance.

After weeks of hot, dry weather, it had begun to rain [redacted] plump droplets splashing on to the pavement [redacted].

People walked [redacted] with shiny faces upturned. [redacted]

[redacted] the nation rejoiced.

[redacted]

[redacted] Day after day after day of the same blue skies is foreign to us. [redacted]

[redacted] The default is grey, a neutral backdrop [redacted]

We are famous for our greyness. [redacted]

[redacted]

Are we the product of our weather?

[redacted] the British climate (rain and fog) [redacted] the British temperament (simple and barbaric).

[redacted]

[redacted] Does precipitation dampen enthusiasm? [redacted]

[redacted]

[redacted] no [redacted].

[redacted]

[redacted] There is no correlation [redacted]

[redacted] And yet.

[redacted] when a watery sun sparkled on puddles [redacted] colours brighter and senses [redacted] keener, [redacted] Don't tell me that is not real.

It is not the heat [redacted] that is un-British. [redacted] it is the invariability. When we pull back the curtains at the start of a new day, we need to be kept guessing [redacted]

Redacted from: https://www.bbc.co.uk/news/uk-45020144

Alice Harvey-Fishenden

Drought

[redacted]

[redacted] bones [redacted]
[redacted] white and dry [redacted]

[redacted]

[redacted]
as breathless [redacted]
[redacted]

[redacted] dust. [redacted]
[redacted] oil and butter
[redacted]

[redacted] singed.

Redacted from: ‘Drought’ by Annette Volfing - First published in 2013 A Commended Poem of the 2013 Stanza Poetry Competition on the theme of 'Drought', judged by Neil Rollinson.

Retrieved from: https://poems.poetrysociety.org.uk/poems/drought/

Jan Hedger

1995 Drought Diary

1995 DROUGHT DIARY

July

[redacted]

[redacted] thunderstorms [redacted] dissolved oxygen [redacted] fish [redacted] virtually obliterated. [redacted] the [redacted] suffering [redacted].

River [redacted] receded [redacted] to [redacted] abstraction.

[redacted]

Redacted from: Spence, R. (1996) Environment Agency 1995 Drought Report – Severn and Trent Catchments

Retrieved from:

www.environmentdata.org/archive/ealit:250/OBJ/19001086.pdf

Jan Hedger

1995 Drought Diary

2.2 1995 Drought Diary

[redacted] refill [redacted] and [redacted] recharge. [redacted] the [redacted]

Spring

[redacted] river flows [redacted] With increasing [redacted] abstractions [redacted]

[redacted] the [redacted] Reservoir [redacted] restricted [redacted] irrigation [redacted] the [redacted] Public [redacted] demands [redacted] garden sprinklers.

Redacted from: Spence, R. (1996) Environment Agency 1995 Drought Report – Severn and Trent Catchments

Retrieved from:

www.environmentdata.org/archive/ealit:250/OBJ/19001086.pdf

Helen Johnson

Redacted Poem based on Siegfried Sassoon's poem 'Haunted'

... louring
drought sucked
baked
brooding
ugly sorrows
shake off dread
sweat of horror
scent of tired men
fading
far-off
churring
night-jar's note
confused
wretched
choking
barbed
clawed
baffling
looping
terror
zigzag
squat
bestial
headlong
roaring agony
groping
strangling

Redacted from: 'Haunted' by Siegfried Sassoon (1886-1967)

Retrieved from: https://poets.org/poem/haunted-0

Sassoon's poem speaks to me of a shrivelled, crushed spirit - the only moisture to be had, perhaps, his own sweat - in a barren landscape - a nightmare; dead trees, charred earth in which he stumbles blindly, looking for life; for meaning. For sustenance. For redemption. Whatever form it takes.

Daralyn Hammond

OTHER DROUGHT POETRY

Various Forms

Drought

The reservoir has been drained
of purpose, of life, of water.
Revealing the past land surface
where once people walked
pooled with stagnant water
where dormant grass resurges.
The water flows to far away
where, safe in their homes
sheltered from the weather,
people pump out water
to pool on their green lawns.

Alice Harvey-Fishenden

Drought

Clouds missing.

Blue skies again

red hot sun burning like chilli peppers.

Crying children that cannot sleep, restless through the night.

Tempers lost with fractious children.

'Sun cream! Hats!' you shout out all the time.

Outside pavements burning hot bring blisters to bare feet.

Grass hard and prickly like a hedgehog's back to bare feet.

All animals hide away from heat.

Plants droop like aging people.

The ponds smell like dirty feet.

Roots of plants in ponds show like long thin toes stretching out.

Goldfish lie at the bottom, gasping for water, is this the end?

Patricia Wardle

Mother Earth

I can see and hear Mother Earth clutching at her dry throat

fish dry-drown in death throes, their mouths gape and gasp in our waterless rivers and streams.

Seas no longer ebb and flow.

Creatures paw the parched soil, frantically pulling up withered brown grass stalks in a futile attempt to retrieve moisture from them.

Insects patiently await the arrival of dawn, yearning for the life-sustaining droplet of dew on the dry, dead branches above them, but it does not come.

Their broken bodies creak like old rusty gates as they scuttle around in their desperate search for life-giving sustenance.

The blue skies are cloudless and there is a bleakness on the horizon as it foretells the stark improbability of any rainfall and the world fades to grey.

Yvonne Ugarte

Reservoir

Bones

bare

breathless

gasp for water

last reserves

of rain

gifted

to man

but now

man attaches

hosepipes

to syphon

of the marrow

whilst Mother

lies parched

and burnt

Claire Hughes

The Desiccated Engineer

He had not thought of this:
a drought.
Had not believed
that his canal
could run out
of water.
Where once
a smooth passage
lay; now clay,
baked dry
and cracked,
the boats
laid up
and backed
all the way
to Milton.
Transport
by means
of water
had been
his dream;
now, it seemed
he must

navigate

his way

to transport

of water

itself.

Wearily,

he turned,

reached up,

shook off

the dust

and took

his plans

from off

the shelf.

Mark Johnson

Commissioned Poem: Deluge

An indigo sky threatens: overcast, foreboding.
We batten down the hatches in readiness for weather forecasters' warnings.
Night falls, sky dances darkly,
storm clouds gather – an eerie congregation in grey.

The first cloud drips a tentative few drops, others erupt - burst open
as if waiting for the signal, and a deluge descends
battering car windscreens, window panes, late night dog walkers caught in the rain.
Rivulets run along road gutters racing to drain.

As Earth rotates, night turns to day,
the dawn breaks into grey and rain continues to c
a
s
c
a
d
e
like sharp arrows plunging into skin where wet faced commuters peer from cagoules
and overnight rainfall closes schools.

Met Office announces a 'red alert' and emergency services dive into action
rescuing a bus driver trapped in his bus in a metre deep water in a lane near Gayton,
rescuing drivers from car roofs as if standing on half sunken tin cans,
guiding terrified sheep tiptoeing on hooves to dry land.

The Trent and Mersey canal overflows

creating a swirling moat around a first school in Stone
where children are carried carefully in strong arms
over streaming rivers of water, away from harm.

Rivers burst banks and meadows of water taunt; tapping and lapping at doors
of homes where residents have moved to upper floors,
placing their faith in sandbags against doorways and gates,
over basement grates.

They can only wait - and contemplate the cause...

Fields turned to housing estates - concrete houses and roads,
not enough natural drainage remaining to absorb the rain's flow?
Litter and man-made debris blocking drains?
Climate change?

It's easy to blame 'the weather'
and grumble ignorant remarks from under umbrellas
but 'the weather' is a natural phenomenon:
nature purely cleansing Mother Earth - responding to rising and falling pressures and weather patterns.

What about our patterns of behaviour, our damaging ways?
We must take responsibility, make a change before it becomes too late.
Respect the Earth and nature's power.
We are merely visitors - the Earth is not ours

to claim,
to
abuse,
to ignore its beauty.

Overhead, a Bow of Promise appears.

Based on the Staffordshire Floods of July 2012

https://www.bbc.co.uk/news/uk-england-stoke-staffordshire-18737376

Mel Wardle Woodend

UK CLIMATE RESILIENCE PROGRAMME

Clandage: Building Climate Resilience Through Community, Landscapes and Cultural Heritage

Background

'Historically, landscapes, communities and people have coped with, and adapted to, environmental change, and continue to do so. This happens both through barely perceptible incremental changes, and also through rapid adjustments to abrupt environmental changes, for instance through landscape loss and gain.

Understanding how communities have adapted to changing circumstances in the past sheds light on how future changes might be managed and communicated, as well as how the resilience of people and their places can be enhanced, at a range of spatial and temporal scales.

However, as past community adaptation is often not well recorded or inaccessible, it is not part of decision making on how to respond to current and future environmental change. This project intends to address this gap.'

For more information, please visit:

https://www.ukclimateresilience.org/projects/clandage-building-climate-resilience-through-community-landscapes-and-cultural-heritage/

DREAM WELL WRITING LTD

Dream Well Writing Ltd are Staffordshire based publishers of dyslexia friendly books – with worldwide distribution and an environmentally conscious ethos – founded in 2017 by Mel Wardle Woodend Staffordshire Poet Laureate 2019 – 2022.

Find out more about Dream Well at

http://dreamwellwriting.simplesite.com/

https://www.facebook.com/dreamwellwriting/

dreamwellwriting@gmail.com

DREAM WELL

Printed in Great Britain
by Amazon

86619665R10048